Single
Married
Separated
&
Life After
Divorce
Workbook

Single
Married
Separated
&
Life After
Divorce
Workbook

By Myles Munroe

Based on the Workbook Compiled by
Dunamis Bible Training Center

Destiny Image® **Publishers, Inc.**
P.O. Box 310
Shippensburg, PA 17257-0310

"Speaking to the Purposes of God for This Generation"

ISBN 1-56043-115-6

For Worldwide Distribution
Printed in the U.S.A.

Third Printing: 1996   Fourth Printing: 1997

This book and all other Destiny Image, Revival Press, and Treasure House books
are available at Christian bookstores and distributors worldwide.

For a U.S. bookstore nearest you, call **1-800-722-6774**.
For more information on foreign distributors, call **717-532-3040**.
Or reach us on the Internet: **http://www.reapernet.com**

For further information on related subject material, write:

Dr. Myles Munroe
Bahamas Faith Ministries International
P.O. Box N-9583
Nassau, Bahamas

Contents

How to Use This Workbook

This workbook has been prepared to help you better understand and grasp the principles discussed in *Single, Married, Separated & Life After Divorce*. Whether you use the workbook for *individual* or *group* study, the following approach will help you get the most out of each chapter.

Preview
- Read the title
- Read the first paragraph and scan the headings
- Read the last paragraph

Question
- Ask yourself how you can apply the subject matter to yourself
- Glance over the workbook questions

Read
- Read the chapter thoroughly
- Try to find answers for the questions you asked yourself
- Watch carefully for answers to workbook questions

Review (for understanding)
- Go over the main points in your mind, or
- Discuss them with your group leader

Recall (for memory)
- Recall the important facts in the chapter
- Recall the main principle(s) discussed

Study
- Complete the workbook questions
- Scan the text for answers
- Reread portions if necessary
- Check your answers with the *Answer Key*

This study format is flexible and may be used for a *group* study in the following manner:

Study Group
Preview
Introduce new chapter

Homework
Read assigned chapter
Answer workbook questions

Study Group
Discussion
Review and Recall

The Review Quiz at the end of the workbook is optional and covers the entire book.

Chapter 1

The Myth of Singleness

It's okay to be single, but not good to be alone.
 1. People do not have a "singleness problem"; they have an entirely different problem called
    _____ _____ .
 2. How does the dictionary describe "singleness"? How does the world view it?

 3. What should be a primary goal of every Christian?

 4. What causes 99 percent of marital problems?

 5. God said it was not good that man should be (*alone/single* circle one).
 6. Did Adam need someone to fulfill him? Why or why not?

 7. Are all unmarried people alone?

 8. How did God answer Adam's situation of being alone?

 9. God (*chooses/presents* circle one) an individual as your mate.
10. Because God chose to give man the right to choose, He

11. What does *alone* mean?

12. Explain how keys on a key ring illustrate singleness.

13. How much does God like uniqueness?

**Being single—separate, unique and whole—is most essential to,
and the foundation of, all relationships.**

Chapter 2

God Wants You to Be Single

Singleness is a state to be pursued, not avoided. To be single should be the goal of every married person.

1. True or False. Until you reach the state of being single, you are not ready to stop being alone.
2. Is it safer to be unmarried if you aren't single? Explain.

3. What is the real key to happiness? Who holds that key?

4. The goal of each Christian, according to the apostle Paul, is

5. What happens when you become too busy looking for someone to be all things to you?

6. When will you be ready for God to present someone to you?

7. What three needs can no other person meet for you?
    1.
    2.
    3.
8. Before you can love your neighbor, who must you love first?

9. What are the first two steps toward wholeness?
    1.
    2.
10. What is the real reason for people gossiping, judging and criticizing?

11. What is the second greatest commandment, according to Jesus?

Your marriage will only be as successful as your singleness.

Chapter 3

The Advantage of Being Unmarried

A successful marriage is only the product of two people being successfully single.

1. You are not yet successful at being single if you cannot

2. Name some people who, while they were single, made some of the greatest contributions to the Kingdom of God. Explain what they did.

3. What freedom do single people have that married people do not?
4. True or False. Everyone could live unmarried for a lifetime.

5. For those who want to marry, what is the best promise in the Scriptures?

6. Which picture best represents a marriage built the right way?

A.

B.

7. What should you build before building a marriage?

If you are unmarried, now is the time to become truly single.

Chapter 4

An Omelet Is Only as Good as the Eggs

Is it not better, however, to begin with *two* good eggs?
1. Explain, in modern terms, the principle in Proverbs 25:28.

2. People who are not yet "separate, whole and unique" because of being founded in Jesus

3. What middle ground should you reach for concerning other people's opinions about you?

4. True or False. Marriage is a 50-50 proposition.
5. What causes the sickness of loneliness?

6. How can you tell whether or not you are a whole person?

7. True or False. No one was born to be married; however, everyone was born not to be alone.
8. List some of the dangerous presumptions concerning marriage that are circulating in the church world.
    1.
    2.
    3.
9. What are some possible reasons for your being attracted to someone?
    2.
    3.

A happily married man or woman is still single.

Chapter 5

Singleness Is God's Joy

A person in a state of being single is a joy to the Lord.
1. Why would God find a special joy in single people?

2. On the other hand, what is one of the doctrines of devils concerning marriage that Paul listed in First Timothy 4:3?

3. God made (*singleness/marriage* circle one) of first importance.
4. Which picture best illustrates a marriage?

A.

B.

5. What is the only thing that binds two people together in a marriage?

6. What part does the Holy Spirit play in your marriage?

7. The word (*disciple/spouse* circle one) is more important to God.

God designed everything in the Kingdom around the individual.

Chapter 6

Prepared for Marriage

Most people do not get prepared; they just get married.

1. What two beliefs do you need in order to choose a life of single-minded focus on Jesus?
    1.
    2.
2. If you know that the unmarried life is not for you, what should you begin to ask God for?

3. Instead of attaching themselves to their spouses, what should husbands and wives do?

4. What the world thinks of as romance is really _____ _____ .
5. What is the result of your losing yourself in someone else?

6. What does it mean to be individual?

7. True or False. You are to keep your identity when you marry.
8. What three ingredients from God ensure a happy marriage?
    1.
    2.
    3.
9. Which married couples cannot be guaranteed eternal love?

10. What is God's plan and context for marriage?

Marriage is "the second level of God's building blocks."

Chapter 7

We Live in Two Worlds

The only people God puts together are two people with the Holy Spirit within them. Everyone else, man marries.

1. Describe the two worlds in which Christians live.

2. From where does the pressure to get married come?

3. Why do unmarried adults feel that they are less than "human"?

4. God did not create _____ but _____ , _____ humans.
5. You are not a "whole, single" being who is prepared for marriage until

6. What "trick" question did the Pharisees ask Jesus?

7. True or False. Being married in a church building does not mean God has put a man and woman together.
8. If two believers are married and want to get a divorce, to whom *should* they go back to get it?

9. How do two born-again people handle marital problems?

10. According to Jesus, why did Moses give the divorce commandment?

11. What is the one cause for breaking apart a marriage in God's world? Explain why.

12. Is a person who has one eye on God and one eye on the opposite sex ready for marriage? Explain.

God joins man and woman in a context of permanence.

Chapter 8

Remain in the Station Where God Called You

True love is not a feeling; it is a choice and a decision.

1. What does "Let every man abide in the same calling wherein he was called" (I Cor. 7:20) say in connection to marriage?

2. Can a married person who is not single seek to become so? How?

3. Jesus' words about being able to live alone as a single person imply that it is a _____ .
4. What two climates undergirded Paul's discussion of the assets and liabilities of marriage?

5. True or False. Being unmarried means having more challenges and responsibilities.
6. In God's context, marriage means making choices

7. In marriage, your body belongs to (*you/your spouse* circle one).
8. According to Paul, what is the only way a husband or wife can deprive a spouse of sexual rights?

Your pursuit in life should not be marriage but singleness.

Chapter 9

Divorce and the Bible

Do what you are called upon to do wherever you are, and do it as unto the Lord.

1. Christians must face divorce and know _____ _____ in various situations involving it, not _____ _____ .

2. What is separation?

3. Why did the disciples feel that it was better not to marry?

4. What are the three categories of people who can live successfully without marrying, according to Jesus?
   1.
   2.
   3.

5. What attitude does most of the world have about marriage? What was marriage's actual intention?

6. Why did Paul write to the Corinthians about the subject of sex?

7. Why should you be careful about activating the appetite of sex?

8. Why should a new believer who is married stay with his or her unbelieving mate?

9. How should a believer respond to an unbelieving mate who wants to leave?

10.   What upholds you and keeps you sane in your circumstances?

11.   What happens to the marriage of most people who marry just because of passion?

12.   Summarize in one sentence Paul's advice to the Corinthians:

Marriage is the death and sacrifice of exclusivity on the altar of love.

Chapter 10

The History of Divorce

When reading the Bible, one of the most dangerous things you can do is isolate verses from their context.

1. Define *context*.

2. What was a teaching method used at the time Jesus taught?

3. What is a hyperbole? Give an example of one.

4. Which of the following are techniques of "wisdom teaching"? Circle the correct answers.

proverbs	figures of speech	examples
repetition	definitions	drawings
questions	parables	numbers
riddles	allegories	hyperbole

5. We need to study the Word according to

6. What are the three principles necessary for correct interpretation of Scripture?
    1.
    2.
    3.
7. True or False. Jesus came to show the people what the law really meant and why it was given.
8. What is the context to Jesus' words about divorce?

9. Divorce is the _____ _____ of _____ _____ .
10. True or False. Jesus removed the spiritual dimension from Moses' law.
11. In Old Testament times, was adultery grounds for divorce? Explain.

12. As Christians, what should we think about? What should we *not* think about?

13. God hates (*divorce/divorcees* circle one) but He loves (*divorce/divorcees* circle one).
14. Why were the "mixed marriages" mentioned in Ezra 10 abandoned? What is the scriptural principle behind that decision?

15. We need to find out from God _____ of His principles or commandments really applies in a situation.

**If marriage is properly understood and entered into, there will be no need
for consideration of divorce.**

Chapter 11

The Husband's Responsibility

From the beginning of the world, God placed the responsibility of marriage on men.

1. What are the two principles given in Genesis 2:24 for men who marry?
   1.
   2.
2. Why does a man leave his parents?

3. What New Testament word was translated as *divorce*? What does it mean in Greek?

4. When a man takes a wife, he is to (*stick to/defect from* circle one) her.
5. In effect, God said, "Divorce rests upon the shoulders of the _____."

6. Whatever happens in the home is the husband's (*responsibility/fault* circle one).
7. What one way out of marriage has God provided?

8. As your _____ was not designed for _____ , so your _____ is not designed for _____ .
9. Which of the following really joins a couple?
   A. love
   B. children
   C. God
   D. spending years together

10. True or False. Some people may be legally married but not joined.
11. Before pursuing a woman, what should a man decide?

12. What should an individual look for in another person when considering marriage?

13. Love cannot subdue a person's _____ .
14. True or False. A submitted body means the same as a submitted will.
15. Marriage is the joining or uniting of two _____ .

Don't make a move unless you're ready to die for the commitment.

Chapter 12

Broken Relationships

If you and I break fellowship, it hurts God worse than it hurts us.

1. What is detrimental to the flow of fellowship?

2. In what form is broken fellowship destructive to a person and to his or her fellowship with God?

3. A broken heart is actually a _____ _____ .
4. The soul is composed of what three things?
   1.
   2.
   3.
5. You _____ a spirit being who _____ a soul and _____ in a body.
6. Attempting to restore a broken relationship can be like what?

7. Who is involved in destroying relationships?

8. What precedes a legal marriage?

9. Explain "soul ties."

10. On what is emotional bonding based?

11. Alienation is:

12. Bonding is never a _____ , but a result of _____ in a relationship.

13. What happens to emotional bonds in a separation?

14. How do you avoid broken relationships?

15. Is it possible to be legally divorced and still be emotionally married? Explain.

16. The moment you _____ to someone, anything that breaks up that relationship is an emotional divorce.

17. What is the difference between separation and divorce?

18. What is the difference between a promise and a vow?

19. Why did God say you should not make a vow if you aren't going to keep it?

20. What does "unto death" mean?

21. In every case, what does emotional divorce produce?

22. What is the good news?

Marriage is not designed for divorce.

Chapter 13

The Traumas of Divorce

A *trauma* is an injury, a wound, or a shock. It amounts to an earthquake to the body, soul or spirit.

1. Traumas cause _____ , which manifests in _____ .
2. What does "being irrational" mean and where does it originate?

3. List the four things that affect a person after a relationship is broken.
    1.
    2.
    3.
    4.
4. When is one of the worst times to make major decisions or to become involved with a possible mate?

5. What does marrying on the rebound do to a person?

6. According to Psalm 18:6, what should you do first when in distress?

7. True or False. Distress involves the same pattern of bereavement that follows a loss in death.
8. True or False. Only positive emotional bonding results in a loss when it is broken.
9. What causes depression?

10. What answer does the Book of Ephesians have for rejection?

11. Name the three basic traumas that result from separation distress.
    1.
    2.
    3.

12.   What is the significance of the phrase "drieth the bones"?

13.   What is emotional suicide?

14.   What is the medicine for these traumas of separation? Include Scripture reference(s).

15.   What is the antidote for the poison of divorce? Include Scripture reference(s).

16.   True or False. The time you feel God is the fartherest is the time He is nearest.
17.   If you are experiencing these feelings and problems, what should you do?

18.   Generally speaking, have churches helped or hindered the recovery of a divorced person? Explain.

There is only one unpardonable sin—and divorce is not it.

Chapter 14

The Aftermath of Trauma

Never confuse who you are with what you have done.

1. How should you *not* measure your self-worth?

2. Measure your _____ _____ by the fact that God gave you _____ before anyone ever met you.
3. Fill in the appropriate information.

    A way to react is: **Which really is:**   **And comes from:**

    1.
    2.
    3.
4. What is the only type of person who handles loss without any unmanageable shaking or ill effects?

5. What is the fourth reaction to trauma?

6. Why is withdrawing into yourself the wrong reaction?

7. What is the danger of attempting to replace pain with people?

8. Instant _____ are no guarantee of instant _____ from pain.
9. After experiencing a separation or divorce, you should take time to back off and

10. After a separation or divorce, people who are not stable in themselves seek desperately for _____ .

11. What happens if emotional wounds are not healed sooner or later?

12.   Explain "maintenance contact."

13.   What steps can you take to regain custody of yourself?
      1.
      2.
14.   From what three sources can you receive counsel?
      1.
      2.
      3.
15.   What is the possible danger in regaining custody of yourself?

16.   Regaining custody of yourself means

Be sure your security is in Christ and the Word for only they will not pass away.

Chapter 15

Emotional Aftershocks

People who have been hurt can be dangerous.
1. To what can the emotional ups and downs of a trauma be compared?

2. Name some emotional aftershocks that can occur.

3. What is the difference between righteous and ungodly anger?

4. *Anger* is a _____ attitude that can cause behavior with _____ effects.
5. What vanishes when panic strikes?

6. Panic always begins with _____ , which usually stems from _____ .
7. Describe an irritable or irate person.

8. Explain the difference between "mood swings" and "mixed feelings."

9. In a breakdown, it is not nerves that actually break down, but a person's

10. What is the progression a person goes through after experiencing a separation or divorce?

11. List the four ways of handling the loss of a relationship.
    1.
    2.
    3.
    4.

12.   What is "openness"?

13.   What requires openness?

14.   You cannot live a _____ _____ and live in the _____.
15.   On what should believers focus?

Let the past be past and move on to the next arena.

Chapter 16

Life After Divorce and Separation

Forgiveness removes any walls between you and God. Forgiveness is vertical as well as horizontal.

1. What is the key to the door to healing?

2. If forgiveness itself does not get rid of the hurt, what does it do?

3. Unforgiveness toward a human being also _____ _____ _____ with God.

4. If your anger has turned to hatred, then you have

5. True or False. When you see someone else as the source of your problem, unforgiveness has gained a foothold in your heart.

6. What is wrong with explaining why you are right before asking for forgiveness?

7. What does it really mean to forgive someone? To ask for forgiveness?

8. A wrong attitude _____ the flow of God's Spirit to you.
9. Forgiveness is (*an emotion/a decision* circle one).
10. True or False. True forgiveness depends on your feelings.
11. What is the requirement for walking in forgiveness and peace in God?

12. An immature Christian can gain maturity through traumatic experiences if

13. What four things did Jesus do that we must do to be spiritually mature?
    1.
    2.
    3.
    4.

14. Wisdom begins in the _____ _____ and through the _____ , but it is expressed through the _____ .

15. What can you do to minimize the chance of triggering other emotional aftershocks?

16. What things should you avoid focusing on after you've gone through a divorce?

17. Solitary healing is being alone with _____ .

18. Allowing others to help you can be called

19. What is the only way to gain victory over life's problems?

20. Identify the elements of the healing process:

_____   _____   D. _____
    A.   B.   C. _____

21. What is the end result of following the healing process?

Without Jesus we can do nothing.

Answer Key

Chapter 1
1. "being single"
2. "To be separate, unique and whole." As "being alone."
3. To be totally single.
4. One or both marriage partners do not see themselves as unique, worthy individuals.
5. alone
6. No. Adam was whole and complete in himself.
7. No.
8. He formed another like Adam to be a companion to him.
9. presents
10. ...limited Himself to only expressing His wishes for us, not making us fulfill His wishes.
11. "exclusive, isolated, solitary"
12. Each key is unique, separate and whole, yet they are joined by the ring. They are single, but not alone.
13. He likes it so much that no two people on earth have identical fingerprints, eye retina patterns, DNA cells, or in men, sperm content.

Chapter 2
1. True
2. Yes. If you do not know your uniqueness or wholeness, then marriage magnifies that lack and you feel trapped.
3. Becoming whole and finding out your uniqueness. God.
4. ..."to be conformed to the image" of Christ (Rom. 8:29).
5. You do not have time to be who you are, and you do not have anything to give.
6. When you get to the place where you do not need anyone else for your life to be whole, unique and separate.
7. 1. ego needs
   2. soul needs
   3. spiritual needs
8. yourself
9. 1. knowing who you are
   2. accepting who you are
10. People feel badly about themselves.
11. To love your neighbor to the same degree that you love yourself (Luke 10:27).

Chapter 3
1. ...control your emotions, your passions, your feelings, your attitudes and your behavior.
2. Corrie ten Boom—Saved many Christians and Jews from the Nazis.
   C.S. Lewis—A great apologist of the Christian faith who wrote many books.

Martin Luther—Restored personal salvation to the Church by discovering justification by faith in the Bible.

John Calvin—A leader in the Reformation.

(May be other answers.)

3. To be concerned only with the things of God.
4. False
5. "But seek ye first the kingdom of God, and His righteousness; and all these things shall be added unto you" (Matt. 6:33).
6. B
7. you

Chapter 4

1. A person who does not know who he or she is becomes fair game for someone else to mold into another image.
2. ...have no roots in themselves.
3. To respect other people's opinions, but not to be moved if people do not see you rightly or try to mold you into their patterns.
4. False
5. Not understanding who you are and being afraid or too proud to make close friends.
6. By seeing how well you keep company with yourself.
7. True
8. 1. "Claiming" a particular person without finding out God's opinion.
   2. "Prophesying" that this person is to marry that person.
   3. Telling a person that "God told me you are going to marry me."
9. 1. sensual feelings
   2. the other person fills an empty area in you
   3. the pressure from the world to get married

Chapter 5

1. God can do more through a person who is satisfied and fulfilled with Him alone.
2. "forbidding to marry"
3. singleness
4. A
5. a covenant
6. He provides the power to enable you to keep your vows.
7. disciple

Chapter 6

1. 1. You are positive you can do it.
   2. You believe it is God's will for you.
2. That He prepare you for marriage.
3. Allow God to bond them together.
4. addictive dependency
5. You either "suck" life from that person, or he or she takes life from you.
6. To be able to be yourself, to have your own opinions and make your own decisions, to come up with your own ideas about things.
7. True
8. 1. God's love
   2. God's Spirit
   3. God's Son, Jesus Christ

9. two married sinners
10. permanence

Chapter 7
1. One is material and under the influence of the satanic world system. The other is supernatural, eternal and under the authority of God.
2. friends, enemies, family, society, media
3. In society's thinking, marriage is a necessary part of adult life.
4. sub-humans; whole, single
5. ...you are prepared never to get a divorce.
6. Whether or not the condition of permanence in marriage applied to everyone.
7. True
8. the preacher
9. Through love and forgiveness and through walking in the fruits of the Spirit.
10. Because of the hardness of the Israelites' hearts.
11. Fornication. It is a direct assault on the physical temple of God.
12. No. A person is totally whole, or single, when both eyes are single-mindedly focused on the Kingdom of God and His righteousness.

Chapter 8
1. If you were unmarried when you became born again, then stay that way until you become truly single. If you were married when you became born again, then stay married.
2. Yes. By seeking God and asking Him to make him or her whole within the context of marriage.
3. gift
4. persecution, promiscuity
5. False
6. ...when you don't feel like it.
7. your spouse
8. By mutually agreeing.

Chapter 9
1. God's will; religious thinking
2. A divorce without legal papers.
3. According to Jesus' teaching, they would not be able to divorce except on the grounds of adultery or fornication (Matt. 5:31-32).
4. 1. Those born without desire or functioning sexual organs.
   2. Those castrated by accident or on purpose.
   3. Those who sacrificed natural desires to serve the Lord single-mindedly.
5. That it is a necessary evil. To be a blessing.
6. He was answering specific requests for advice about some local situations (I Cor. 7:1).
7. Once it is activated, a hunger develops that lasts until you are old.
8. It may be the only access God has to the unbelieving spouse; you could win him or her to Christ by your example.
9. He or she should let the person go.
10. The peace of the Holy Spirit.
11. It eventually will be destroyed.
12. Don't jump into marriage until you make sure you have what it takes to make the marriage work.

Chapter 10
1. The surroundings of an element like a verse: who is speaking, who is being addressed, the subject under discussion, the reason for the discussion, etc.
2. wisdom teaching

3. An exaggeration for effect. Example: "He is as strong as an ox."
4. proverbs, riddles, figures of speech, parables, allegories, examples, hyperbole
5. ...sound principles of interpretation.
6.   1. Keep in mind the literal aspect of the passage.
      2. Find the historical setting of the passage.
      3. Consider the context of the passage.
7. True
8. Jesus was saying that what a person thinks is as important as what he or she does.
9. symptomatic manifestation; marital deficiency
10. False
11. No. Adultery resulted in the person being stoned to death.
12. What makes a marriage. Conditions by which one could get a divorce.
13. divorce; divorcees
14. Spiritual incompatibility. "Be ye not unequally yoked together with unbelievers: for what fellowship hath righteousness with unrighteousness? and what communion hath light with darkness?" (II Cor. 6:14)
15. which

Chapter 11
1.   1. Leave mother and father.
      2. Cleave to the woman you marry.
2. For the cause of he and a woman being in the will of God and in fellowship with God and with one another.
3. *Apostasion.* "A defection"; literally, "a standing off from."
4. stick to
5. husband
6. responsibility
7. death
8. body; worry; marriage; divorce
9. C
10. True
11. That she is "chaseable to the grave."
12. attitude, character, inner spirit being
13. will
14. False
15. souls

Chapter 12
1. separation
2. any form
3. broken soul
4.   1. mind
      2. will
      3. emotions
5. are; has; lives
6. Trying to conquer a fortified city.
7. the thief, satan
8. an emotional marriage
9. They are emotional bonds, where one becomes dependent on another emotionally.
10. time spent together, communication, sharing of hopes, dreams, inner thoughts

11. A kind of family relationship where individuals are related but not bonded.
12. gift; impact
13. They are uprooted or tore out of both parties, like roots being yanked out of the ground.
14. By being careful about your emotional bonding.
15. Yes. A legal divorce only separates a couple in the eyes of the law. It does not separate emotional bonds.
16. commit
17. Separation is the termination of a commitment with emotional involvement. Divorce is legalized separation.
18. A promise is a commitment to do something later. A vow is a binding commitment to begin doing something immediately and to continue to do it for the duration of the vow.
19. It is unto death.
20. You give God the right to allow you to die if you break the vow.
21. a broken heart
22. There is life after divorce.

Chapter 13

1. distress; anxiety
2. It means a person acts without thinking properly; it originates from anxiety.
3. 1. pain
   2. sense of loss
   3. scarring
   4. handicapping
4. Immediately after a separation or divorce.
5. It sets up him or her for a second trauma of separation.
6. Call upon the Lord.
7. True
8. False
9. Contrasting how you thought things were going to be the rest of your life and how they apparently will be after divorce; also from feeling rejected.
10. "...He hath made us accepted in the beloved" (Eph. 1:6).
11. 1. a broken heart
    2. a crushed spirit
    3. a painful soul
12. The bones are the factory for blood; blood is the source of life. Anything that touches the blood, touches a person's very life and existence.
13. It is when a person decides to never have a relationship with anyone again.
14. a cheerful or merry heart (Prov. 15:13; 17:22).
15. Put your hope in God and praise Him (Ps. 43:5).
16. True
17. Take control of them, turn them over to Jesus, and let Him heal you.
18. Hindered. Churches tend to reject and cold shoulder a divorced person because of a religious mind-set.

Chapter 14

1. By whether or not you made mistakes or failed.
2. personal worth; value
3. 1. to withdraw/pride/rejection, depression, great hurt
   2. to be a "social butterfly"/getting even/anger
   3. to jump to another rock/double-mindedness/fear, panic

4. Those whose foundation is Jesus.
5. to become truly independent
6. It is counter-productive to healing because you isolate yourself from help.
7. The potential for falling into another relationship that would fail like the first.
8. relationships; relief
9. ...see what your contribution was to the failed relationship.
10. stabilization
11. Death will eventually result.
12. It is two people who have a broken relationship still keeping in touch with one another.
13. 1. Accept the situation.
     2. Get counsel before making decisions.
14. 1. the Word
     2. the Holy Spirit
     3. people you trust
15. Isolating yourself from all other people.
16. ...you take responsibility for restoring your life according to God's principles and submit to His healing process; to take your roots out of others and yet being able to share your fruit with them.

Chapter 15

1. earthquake aftershocks or waves
2. numbness, anger, self-pity, panic, fear, irritability, mood swings
3. Righteous anger allows you to make right decisions and do right things; ungodly anger causes you to do all the wrong things.
4. temporary; permanent
5. reason
6. fear; insecurity
7. He or she is on the verge of anger, just waiting for a trigger to be pulled.
8. "Mood swings" usually fluctuate between highs and lows; "mixed feelings" waver between love and hate.
9. ...mental capacity to deal with things.
10. numbness, reactions based on emotional shock waves, then recovery or chronic emotional sickness
11. 1. Avoid facing the situation.
     2. Escape the situation.
     3. Deny what happened.
     4. Face facts, accept reality, move into openness to deal with it.
12. An honest desire to face the truth and deal with change.
13. Accepting the event and learning how to go on.
14. healthy life; past
15. On Jesus, and His purpose for their lives.

Chapter 16

1. forgiveness
2. It opens you up to the One who can heal the hurt.
3. blocks your fellowship
4. ...judged someone else and are blaming them.
5. True
6. You have not really expressed any true sorrow or repentance; if the same situation arose again, you would do the exact same thing over again.
7. When you forgive someone, you release that person from whatever you were holding them accountable for. When you ask forgiveness, you admit accountability, expressing sorrow for your behavior. You ask the other to release you from what the other holds you accountable for.

8. blocks
9. a decision
10. False
11. maturity
12. ...he or she will follow the Word.
13.   1. He grew physically.
      2. He increased in wisdom.
      3. He increased in favor with God.
      4. He found favor with His fellow man.
14. spirit being; Word; mind
15. Take care of your body; eat right.
16. on yourself, on problems of living alone, on what other people think, on a new relationship
17. God
18. ...community healing.
19. Going to Jesus and really letting Him have the problems.
20.   A. forgiveness
      B. openness
      C. solitary healing
      D. community healing
21. maturity, balance, true singleness

Review Quiz

True or False

1. _____ It is guaranteed that if you marry just because of passion, your marriage will eventually be destroyed.
2. _____ In marriage, you don't have to share everything with your mate.
3. _____ Once you marry, your time, attention and body are no longer your own.
4. _____ Jesus taught that marriage is for everyone.
5. _____ Separation is a divorce without the legal paperwork.
6. _____ Marriage is the answer to being alone.
7. _____ If you receive Christ after you're married, it is best if you divorce and become single again.
8. _____ When you are hurting, you should check your social thermometer and give out to others in trouble what you need.
9. _____ All unmarried people are alone.
10. _____ You can have your eye on God and on the opposite sex and still be single-minded.
11. _____ Moses gave the divorce commandment because of the hardness of the people's heart.
12. _____ It is possible to be legally divorced and still emotionally married.
13. _____ A man should decide that a woman is worth chasing to the grave before he marries her.
14. _____ Many times divorce is a blessing to an unbeliever.
15. _____ Divorce is always the husband's fault.
16. _____ You are not prepared for marriage until you are prepared to never divorce.
17. _____ Married sinners are joined together by God because He ordains the courts.
18. _____ To choose God instead of a mate is a higher calling.
19. _____ In the Bible, singleness came before marriage.
20. _____ Loneliness is a sickness.
21. _____ "Thou shalt marry" is a command found in the Bible.
22. _____ Marriage is a 50-50 proposition where each partner depends upon the other to complete a whole.
23. _____ You need to get married in order to meet your ego, soul and spiritual needs.
24. _____ Love can subdue a person's will.
25. _____ If you need to get married to be fulfilled or loved, you are not ready for marriage.
26. _____ To be single should be the goal of every married person.
27. _____ God has hand-picked only one person in the world just for you.
28. _____ A successful marriage is only the product of two people being successfully single.
29. _____ God said it was not good for Adam to be single, so He made Eve as a help mate.
30. _____ Your feelings tell you whether or not you can forgive someone.

Completion

1. Name one reason a believer should stay with an unbelieving mate who wishes to stay married.

2. You should build up _____ before building a marriage.
3. What are six descriptive statements or adjectives that would describe a truly single individual?

    _____   _____
    _____   _____
    _____   _____

4. What three ingredients from God ensure a happy marriage?

5. List the steps a person takes to recover from a separation or divorce.

6. Marriage is the joining or uniting of two _____ .
7. List at least five different views concerning singleness, marriage, separation and divorce that you have personally changed in your own mind since completing this workbook.

Multiple Choice
1. _____ Love is:
    A. a warm feeling
    B. a sensual attraction to another
    C. a conscious decision
    D. a subject for novels
2. _____ Panic is:
    A. fear in action
    B. a nervous rising of adrenaline for success
    C. what God does when we sin
    D. a way to release tension
3. _____ A sound mind means:
    A. taking two aspirin
    B. having a whole week without kids
    C. being intellectually educated and smart
    D. correct thinking without fear
4. _____ The door of openness is:
    A. a very friendly feeling toward all people
    B. an honest desire to face the truth
    C. an entrance for sin and emotional sickness to enter your life
    D. an unlocked door
5. _____ Solitary healing is:
    A. isolating yourself from people in self-protection
    B. sitting in a garden to watch nature
    C. spending time alone with God
    D. watching television with your friends

Matching

1.	_____ Separation	A. The death of exclusivity for love
2.	_____ Marriage	B. To exaggerate something for effect
3.	_____ Mixed Marriage	C. Spending time alone with God
4.	_____ Death	D. A lack in completeness; or, to forsake
5.	_____ Soul Ties	E. One responsible for the marriage
6.	_____ Trauma	F. A divorce without legal papers
7.	_____ Alone	G. God's only way out of a marriage
8.	_____ Solitary Healing	H. Relationship of incompatible spirits
9.	_____ Irate	I. Keeping you and yours to yourself
10.	_____ Singleness	J. Emotional bonding
11.	_____ Exclusivity	K. Being separate, unique and whole
12.	_____ Divorce	L. Exclusive, isolated and solitary
13.	_____ Defect	M. On the verge of anger
14.	_____ Hyperbole	N. Earthquake-like shock to your soul
15.	_____ Husband	O. Termination of a marital vow

Review Quiz Answer Key

True or False
1. True
2. False
3. True
4. False
5. True
6. False
7. False
8. True
9. False
10. False
11. True
12. True
13. True
14. True
15. False
16. True
17. False
18. True
19. True
20. True
21. False
22. False
23. False
24. False
25. True
26. True
27. False
28. True
29. False
30. False

Completion
1. Children are affected by the sanctification of the believer. Or, to be a witness of salvation to the unbelieving mate.
2. yourself
3. unique, whole, separate, self-sufficient, independent, single-minded, complete, Kingdom-focused, balanced
4. God's love, God's Spirit, God's Son

5. forgiveness; openness; solitary healing; community healing
6. souls
7. Personalized responses. Answers will vary.

Multiple Choice
1. C
2. A
3. D
4. B
5. C

Matching
1. F
2. A
3. H
4. G
5. J
6. N
7. L
8. C
9. M
10. K
11. I
12. O
13. D
14. B
15. E

Other *exciting titles* by Myles Munroe

UNDERSTANDING YOUR POTENTIAL

This is a motivating, provocative look at the awesome potential trapped within you, waiting to be realized. This book will cause you to be uncomfortable with your present state of accomplishment and dissatisfied with resting on your past success.
Paperback Book, 168p. ISBN 1-56043-046-X Retail $8.99

RELEASING YOUR POTENTIAL

Here is a complete, integrated, principles-centered approach to releasing the awesome potential trapped within you. If you are frustrated by your dreams, ideas, and visions, this book will show you a step-by-step pathway to releasing your potential and igniting the wheels of purpose and productivity.
Paperback Book, 182p. ISBN 1-56043-072-9 Retail $8.99

MAXIMIZING YOUR POTENTIAL

Are you bored with your latest success? Maybe you're frustrated at the prospect of retirement. This book will refire your passion for living! Learn to maximize the God-given potential lying dormant inside you through the practical, integrated, and penetrating concepts shared in this book. Go for the max—die empty!
Paperback Book, 196p. ISBN 1-56043-105-9 Retail $8.99

IN PURSUIT OF PURPOSE

Best-selling author Myles Munroe reveals here the key to personal fulfillment: purpose. We must pursue purpose because our fulfillment in life depends upon our becoming what we were born to be and do. *In Pursuit of Purpose* will guide you on that path to finding purpose.
Paperback Book, 168p. ISBN 1-56043-103-2 Retail $8.99

POTENT QUOTES

Dr. Myles Munroe believes that every day is a classroom, every experience a lesson, and everyone we meet a teacher. In this collection he has taken the life-changing potent sayings and lessons he has learned and powerfully encapsulated them in quote form. Here you'll learn about leadership, ability, potential, and purpose—all in *Potent Quotes*.
Paperback Book, 80p. ISBN 1-56043-161-X (6" X 4") Retail $4.99

Available at your local Christian bookstore.

Internet: http://www.reapernet.com

Prices subject to change without notice.

Other exciting audiotapes
by Myles Munroe

MAXIMIZING YOUR POTENTIAL
12 tapes   ISBN 1-56043-907-6   Retail $58.00

PRINCIPLES OF PURPOSE
8 tapes   ISBN 1-56043-908-4   Retail $42.00

PURPOSE FOR THE FEMALE (MAN)
10 tapes   ISBN 1-56043-910-6   Retail $48.00

PURPOSE FOR THE MALE (MAN)
8 tapes   ISBN 1-56043-911-4   Retail $42.00

PURPOSE FOR THE MAN AND CREATION
4 tapes   ISBN 1-56043-909-2   Retail $25.00

RELEASING YOUR POTENTIAL
10 tapes   ISBN 1-56043-906-8   Retail $48.00

UNDERSTANDING YOUR POTENTIAL
10 tapes   ISBN 1-56043-905-X   Retail $48.00

If not available at your local Christian bookstore, please call
Bahamas Faith Ministries
at 809-341-6444
or call
Destiny Image Publishers
at 1-800-722-6774

Internet: http://www.reapernet.com

Prices subject to change without notice.

Other *exciting titles* by T.D. Jakes

WOMAN, THOU ART LOOSED!

This book offers healing to hurting single mothers, insecure women, and battered wives; and hope to abused girls and women in crisis! Hurting women around the nation—and those who minister to them—are devouring the compassionate truths in Bishop T.D. Jakes' *Woman, Thou Art Loosed!*
Paperback Book, 210p. ISBN 1-56043-100-8 Retail $9.99

WOMAN, THOU ART LOOSED! WORKBOOK

Whether studying in a group or as an individual, this workbook will help you learn and apply the truths found in *Woman, Thou Art Loosed!* If you're searching to increase your spiritual growth, then this workbook is for you.
Paperback Book, 48p. ISBN 1-56043-810-X (8¹ᐟ²" X 11") Retail $6.99

NAKED AND NOT ASHAMED

With a powerful anointing, Bishop T.D. Jakes challenges us to go below the surface and become completely and honestly vulnerable before God and man. In relationships, in prayer, in ministry—we need to be willing to be open and transparent. Why do we fear? God already knows us, but He cannot heal our hidden hurts unless we expose them to Him. Only then can we be *Naked and Not Ashamed*!
Paperback Book, 156p. ISBN 1-56043-835-5 (6" X 9") Retail $11.99

NAKED AND NOT ASHAMED WORKBOOK

This is no ordinary workbook! A companion to *Naked and Not Ashamed*, this "Application Journal" has been carefully created to help you grasp and apply the principles found in the book. In it you'll be asked to do more than mark answers. You'll be called upon to grapple with difficult issues—because God is determined to make you whole, strong, and anointed in His service!
Paperback Book, 56p. ISBN 1-56043-259-4 (8¹ᐟ²" X 11") Retail $6.99

CAN YOU STAND TO BE BLESSED?

You ask God to bless you and difficulties arise. Why? This book will release the hidden strength within you to go on in God, fulfilling the destiny He has for you. The way to this success is full of twists and turns, yet you can make it through to incredible blessing in your life. The only question left will be, *Can You Stand to Be Blessed?*
Paperback Book, 196p. ISBN 1-56043-801-0 Retail $9.99

CAN YOU STAND TO BE BLESSED? WORKBOOK

Are you ready to unlock the inner strength to go on in God? This workbook will help you apply the book's principles to your life. Appropriate for individual or small group study.
Paperback Book, 48p. ISBN 1-56043-812-6 (8¹ᐟ²" X 11") Retail $6.99

Available at your local Christian bookstore.

Internet: http://www.reapernet.com

Prices subject to change without notice.

Other

Destiny Image titles
you will enjoy reading

BLACK COP: THE REAL DEAL

by Richard Lewis.

Decorated more than 70 times for bravery, Detective Richard Lewis depended on his faith when patrolling the dark streets of New York City. With riveting, true-life experiences he tells of the battles against racism that black cops face within the police department. Don't miss this gripping, personal story of New York's most decorated cop—*Black Cop: The Real Deal.*

Hardback Book, 260p. ISBN 1-56043-583-6 (6" X 9") Retail $9.99

IMAGE IS EVERYTHING

by Marvin L.Winans.

Yes, image IS everything! Does the image God has of you match the image you have of yourself? Society today suffers many social ills because of its lack of vision. Without an image we aimlessly grope about in life when we need to focus on what is true and accurate. We need the image that points us in the right direction—because *Image Is Everything*!

Paperback Book, 168p. ISBN 1-56043-262-4 (6" X 9") Retail $10.99

LADY IN WAITING

by Debby Jones and Jackie Kendall.

This is not just another book for singles! With humor, honesty, and biblical truths, the authors help point women to *being* the right woman and not just finding the right man! With *Lady in Waiting*, any woman—married or single—will learn that only a relationship with Jesus will satisfy!

Paperback Book, 196p. ISBN 1-56043-848-7 Retail $8.99

DON'T DIE IN THE WINTER...

by Dr. Millicent Thompson.

Why do we go through hard times? Why must we suffer pain? In *Don't Die in the Winter...* Dr. Thompson explains the spiritual seasons and cycles that people experience. A spiritual winter is simply a season that tests our growth. We need to endure our winters, for in the plan of God, spring always follows winter!

Paperback Book, 168p. ISBN 1-56043-558-5 Retail $7.99

Available at your local Christian bookstore.

Internet: http://www.reapernet.com

Prices subject to change without notice.